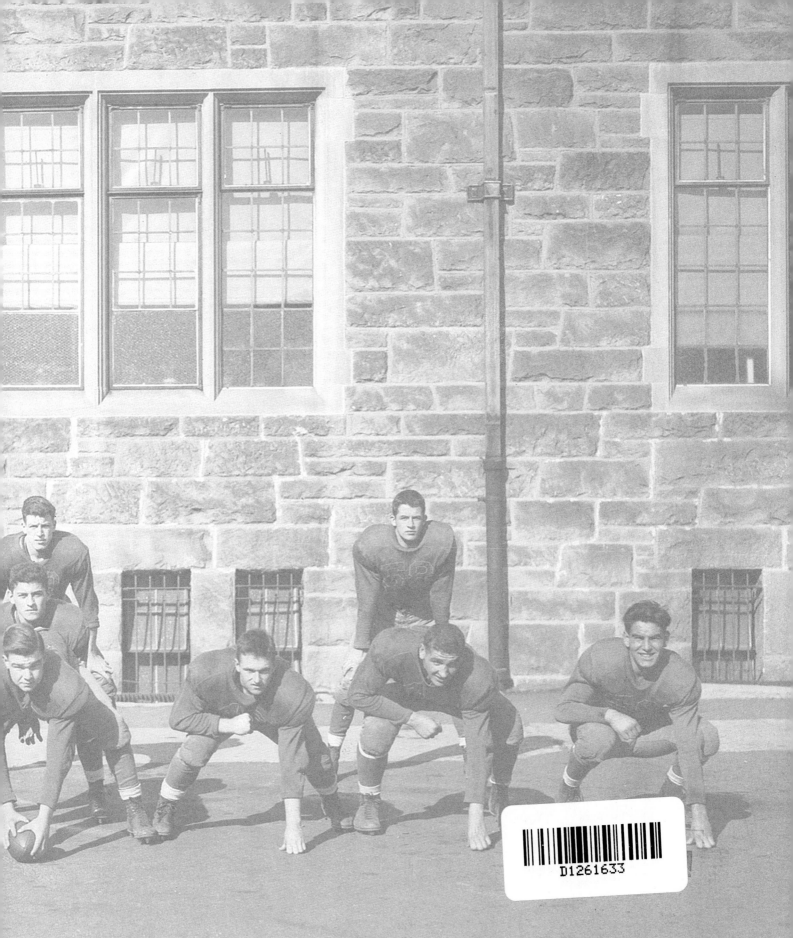

LOMBARDI
An Illustrated Life

Chris Havel

Published by

Krause Publications, a division of F+W Media, Inc.
700 East State Street • Iola, WI 54990-0001
715-445-2214 • 888-457-2873
www.krausebooks.com

To order books or other products call toll-free 1-800-258-0929
or visit us online at www.krausebooks.com or www.Shop.Collect.com

Front Cover Photo:
Vince Lombardi carried off field in victory after the 1961 NFL Championship game.
Marvin E. Newman/Sports Illustrated/Getty Images

Book Back Cover and Title Page Photo:
Lombardi at his desk in his Green Bay office, 1967. Vernon Biever/Getty Images
Lombardi on the sidelines. Focus on Sport/Getty Images

Slipcase Back Cover Photo:
Lombardi family, 1959
AP Photo/Martin Cohn

Contents Page Photo:
Lombardi on the sidelines in 1967 against the Cleveland Browns.
AP Photo/Paul Shane

ISBN-13: 978-1-4402-1809-5
ISBN-10: 1-4402-1809-9

Cover Design by Kevin Ulrich
Designed by Kevin Ulrich
Edited by Paul Kennedy

Printed in China

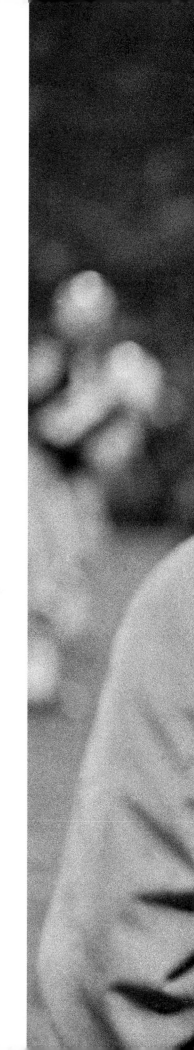

CONTENTS

THE PURSUIT OF EXCELLENCE

BY BART STARR

ONE OF MY FAVORITE QUOTES comes from William Jennings Bryan, who said, "Destiny is not a matter of chance. It is a matter of choice: It is not something to be wished for, it is something to be achieved."

That eloquently states Coach Lombardi's philosophy.

Coach Lombardi believed, as I do, that we have a moral obligation to use our God-given talents to their fullest. We have an obligation to ourselves, our family and our country to strive to reach our potential.

This message rings true today, just like it did in the 1960s.

It is why Coach Lombardi's beliefs and his teachings—his very essence—continue to captivate the curious and motivate the converted. His genius wasn't pointing out what we needed to do to be successful. His genius was motivating us to take the leap from "knowing" to "doing."

Coach Lombardi showed me that by working hard and studying diligently, I could overcome my weakness to the point where I could be one of the best. Absolutely, it was difficult at times because he'd jump right down your throat. He didn't do it in a brutal, nasty way. (I don't mean it like that). He was just tough. That was him. We understood that and we accepted it. I was never upset with him for being overly harsh or tough like that. That wasn't his objective. It was simply to make the point: Here was his technique in doing it.

I came to appreciate the bluntness and unique talent Coach had for teaching and re-emphasizing in the practice sessions. If you did something extremely well in practice, he'd say, "That's just what we're looking for." If you made a mistake he was quick and sharp to correct it, "Now wait a minute, damn it, we WILL NOT do such and such." You came to appreciate his thoroughness.

Coach Lombardi was a fabulous leader. This man was rigidly prioritized: it was God, family and others, and the Green Bay Packers fell under the word "others" and I mean it. That's how

he lived. If you were not in a football meeting, he didn't talk about football. He talked about life. Whenever he was with someone you could see the total person, which was continually emphasized by him.

I think the most meaningful thing he ever said to me was actually in his first meeting with us as a team when he came to Green Bay. He held what today would be likened to a mini-camp session. It was in spring and was primarily a classroom session. He opened the meeting by THANKING THE GREEN BAY PACKERS for the opportunity. That immediately told us a great deal about the quality of this man. We were seated at tables when he walked up to us and said, "Gentlemen, we are going to relentlessly chase perfection knowing full well we won't catch it because nothing is perfect. We are going to RELENTLESSLY— and he really hammered the word RELENTLESSLY—chase perfection because in the process we will catch excellence.

He paused for a moment, walked even closer to us, and said, "I'm not remotely interested in being just good."

Now that's how he opens the session. Wow! We didn't even need a chair to sit in, we were so crouched and poised and primed. We could have been there without a seat the rest of the day.

Those who did not want to, or who were reluctant to follow his guidelines and understand his principles of how it was always TEAM first, weren't around very long.

It has been more than 40 years since Coach Lombardi passed away, but his popularity continues and his message endures. Coach Lombardi's legacy lives on because he was a man who did not leave destiny to chance.

AP photo

A 17th round draft choice in 1956, Bart Starr became one of the game's greatest quarterbacks under Lombardi. Starr led the Packers to five NFL and two Super Bowl championships in the 1960s. He was inducted into the Pro Football Hall of Fame in 1977.

1

FAITH, FAMILY AND FOOTBALL

VINCENT THOMAS LOMBARDI was born June 11, 1913, in Sheepshead Bay, Brooklyn.

The eldest son of Harry and Matilda Lombardi was given his paternal grandfather's name, in the Italian tradition, followed by a very strict but loving upbringing in the Catholic Church, also in the Italian tradition.

The Lombardi's modest, two-story home at 2542 East Fourteenth Street in Sheepshead Bay was the center of young Vinnie's universe.

His father, Harry, was a butcher. He and Vinnie's uncle Eddie owned a wholesale meat shop on the Hudson River waterfront. The business enabled Harry to provide life's necessities for his family, which grew to seven with the arrivals of Madeline, Harold, Claire and Joe.

Harry was born Enrico Lombardi in Italy in 1890, and arrived in New York at age 2. He grew up exploring the rough-

---

"THE QUALITY OF A PERSON'S LIFE IS IN DIRECT PROPORTION TO THEIR COMMITMENT TO EXCELLENCE, REGARDLESS OF THEIR CHOSEN FIELD OF ENDEAVOR."

-Vince Lombardi

Lombardi's youth was dominated by religion, family and sports. Here he is (third from right, top row) with the priests of St. Mark's Parish and neighborhood boys. *Courtesy Green Bay Packers Hall of Fame*

and-tumble streets of lower Manhattan, and profited from that education. Harry learned to become tough, frugal and disciplined—a self-made man like so many of America's first-generation immigrants—whose philosophy was simple, direct and no-nonsense: If you can't afford it, don't buy it.

Harry's beliefs were shaped by a difficult childhood. His father, Vincent, died when Harry was in grade school. Harry quit school after the fifth grade and went to work in a butcher shop to help support the family. It was a man's job that included handling heavy sides of meat and cutting up beef and pork carcasses. Harry made the most of his circumstances by learning the meat business, becoming a butcher and saving enough money to open his and Eddie's shop.

Vinnie's mother, Matilda (Matty), was the Brooklyn-born daughter of Antonio and Loretta (Laura) Izzo, who came to America as teenage immigrants from southern Italy.

Antonio, whose nickname was "Tony the Barber," owned Izzo's Barber Shop, which was located at the corner of East Sixteenth

and Sheepshead Bay Road. The shop doubled as an unofficial clearinghouse for inside information on the local thoroughbred racing scene. Tony the Barber's regulars included jockeys, owners, trainers and bookies from the local track. A racing tip was as frequesnt as a shave.

Antonio and Laura raised 13 children—eight boys and five girls—most of whom married and settled near their parents' house at East Sixteenth Street.

Matty, the Izzo's third child, completed her formal education through the eighth grade. After that, she became a stay-at-home nanny to help her parents look after her brothers and sisters.

That changed when Harry's friend and barber, Frank Izzo, introduced Harry to his sister, Matilda. After a brief courtship they were married on September 5, 1912. They rented an apartment for several years before buying a home two blocks from Matty's parents.

The Izzos boasted more than 50 families in close proximity, and by all accounts they were considered Sheepshead Bay royalty.

At the center of Vince Lombardi's world filled with cousins, aunts, uncles and grandparents were his parents, Harry and Matilda (seated center). *Courtesy Green Bay Packers Hall of Fame*

OPPOSITE: Lombardi's passion for the controlled violence of football found a receptive home at Fordham University. *Courtesy Fordham University Archives*

The large extended family afforded young Vinnie a far-reaching safety net woven from the fabric of cousins, aunts, uncles and grandparents.

When Vinnie wasn't attending mass at St. Mark's Catholic Church, he was working for his father or playing with friends. In the summer, Manhattan and Brighton beach were the place to be. The streets and boardwalks were filled with New Yorkers in search of fun. Vinnie not only played at Brighton Beach as a youngster, but later worked summer jobs there as a lifeguard, security guard and janitor.

Vinnie attended grade school at P.S. 206—a lengthy hike from his home—and displayed leadership skills even at a young age. He was the one organizing games, choosing teams and directing the action.

Vinnie loved to compete, hated to lose and was passionate to the core. Whether it was a game of Hearts or baseball was irrelevant. Vinnie wanted to win and played accordingly, although his childhood was anything but all fun and games.

His father was demanding, especially where his eldest son was concerned. Harry insisted that Vinnie strive for perfection whether the task was great or small. There was only one way to do things, Harry would tell Vinnie, and that was the right way. That message was delivered directly, loudly and often harshly. Corporal punishment was a given in the Lombardi household.

In this disciplined world, one filled with responsibility, the pursuit of excellence and a large, devoutly Catholic family, Vinnie's two great passions—God and football—took root.

The Church was not some distant institution to be visited once a week, but part of the rhythm of daily life for the family. When his mother baked bread, it was one for the Lombardis, and one for the priests, which Vinnie shuttled down the block to St Mark's Rectory. Fr. Daniel J. McCarthy, pastor at St. Mark's, was a frequent dinner guest and often took Vinnie and his friends to baseball games and excursions to Coney Island.

Vinnie had a keen desire to serve as an altar boy at St. Mark's. That longing to assist the priest during services led Vinnie to a critical juncture in his life. Only 12 and serving at Easter Mass, Vinnie heard a calling to the priesthood. In a strict Catholic family such a calling was taken seriously.

Competing for his devotion, however, was football. The game's strategy and physicality appealed to Vinnie from the outset, becoming the first secular love of his life. He played sandlot football at every opportunity. He enjoyed watching football almost as much as he delighted in playing it. When possible he would coax friends to accompany him to the Polo Grounds to see New York's professional football Giants play, or to watch the top college teams.

Vince's thoughts seldom strayed far from football. Years later, Lombardi explained his love of the sport. "Contact, controlled violence, a game where the mission was to hit someone harder, knees up, elbows out, challenge your body, mind and spirit, exhaust yourself and seek redemption through fatigue, such were the rewards an altar boy found in his favorite game."

Though wondrous to a young man, the rewards of football also presented a bit of a quandary.

At age 15, Vince graduated from P.S. 206. He was a good but not great student, and he faced a difficult decision. Where should he continue his education? Ultimately, he chose to enroll as a high school freshman at Cathedral College of the Immaculate Conception, which locals shortened to Cathedral Prep, a pre-seminary operated by the Catholic Diocese of Brooklyn for boys intending to enter the priesthood.

Vince spent three years at Cathedral Prep, schooled in traditional courses, but also required to take Latin and Greek. He was a solid B+ student, popular with classmates. He played baseball and basketball, but athletic opportunities were few at Cathedral Prep, an institution whose singular purpose was to produce priests, not athletes.

In June of 1932, Vince finished his final exams and left Cathedral Prep, deciding a life in the priesthood was not for him. He rarely spoke about the decision, and when asked about it later in life, he declined comment.

Vince moved on to St. Francis Prep in Brooklyn, playing football on a scholarship that covered $150 in fees for books and tuition. He parlayed that experience into a high school diploma and a college athletic scholarship.

Vince's timing could not have been better. St. Francis was in the midst of upgrading its football program, and the decision to enroll there made sense. St. Francis coveted good students and good football players. Vince was both.

Vince was a two-way star who played guard and halfback on offense, and a lineman on defense. He was a supremely effective short-yardage runner and a more than willing blocker. He also was regarded as a skilled, tenacious tackler on defense. He led a defense that allowed just 20 points in six games.

St. Francis lost its season opener, but rebounded to win five straight and tie for the best record among New York's private schools. The team's success and Vince's contributions garnered attention. Columbia offered him a football scholarship, but he preferred to attend a Catholic institution. So he asked Dan Kern, a Fordham University graduate who taught at St. Francis, if he would be willing to write a letter of recommendation. Fordham athletics director Jack Coffey responded with an invitation for Vince to make an on-campus visit. It didn't take long for Vince to receive and accept a football scholarship.

With that, young Vince Lombardi's course was charted.

LOMBARDI ARRIVED at Fordham University in the summer of 1933 a 20 year-old freshman eager to tackle both the academic and athletic challenges that awaited him.

In the classroom, Lombardi proved to be a conscientious, hard-working student who took his studies seriously. He was not brilliant in the classic academic sense, but he was thorough, thoughtful and competitive. He also showed an interest in teaching—which is coaching in a classroom—when he chose to tutor fellow students during his college days.

Although grades didn't come easily to Lombardi, he cared deeply, stayed with it and ultimately graduated in the top 25 percent of his class. Among football players, he was in the top 10 percent, no small feat at such a demanding institution of higher learning.

Those who knew him weren't surprised. Jim Lawlor, Lombardi's close friend and roommate, observed in Michael O'Brien's 1987 biography, *Vince*, that "Anything Vince did (at Fordham), he did wholeheartedly."

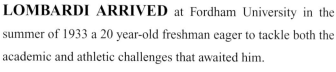

"THE MEASURE OF WHO WE ARE
IS WHAT WE DO WITH WHAT WE HAVE."
-*Vince Lombardi*

Wellington Mara, who graduated *cum laude* and went on to become owner of the New York Giants, noted that his friend "was darn well sure he was going to get what he went after."

Lombardi's determined attitude was reflected not only in the classroom but on the football field. The 5-foot-9, 180-pound guard was undersized and occasionally underestimated because of it. It was a mistake discerning opponents rarely made twice.

His squat build placed limitations on Lombardi's agility and speed, but it also featured powerful shoulders and thick forearms and wrists that enabled him to neutralize foes with an explosive, compact "punch."

Lombardi hoped to play fullback at Fordham, but almost immediately the Rams' coaching staff determined he lacked the speed to be anything beyond an effective short-yardage ball carrier.

Fortunately, Fordham head coach Jim Crowley and his staff also recognized a good football player when they spied one. After only a few practices Lombardi was inserted into the starting

Lombardi (40) pursues a Purdue ball carrier during a game against Fordham. Frank Leahy, Fordham's line coach, said about Lombardi: "There never was a more aggressive man who played for me." Also pictured playing for Purdue is Cecil Isbell (88) who would play for the Green Bay Packers from 1938 to 1942. *Photo by Fordham University/Getty Images*

BELOW: The Seven Blocks of Granite formed the foundation of Fordham football as it rose to college football prominence. From left: John Druze, Al Babartsky, Vince Lombardi, Alex Wojciechowicz, Natty Pierce, Ed Franco and Leo Paquin. *Courtesy Green Bay Packers Hall of Fame*

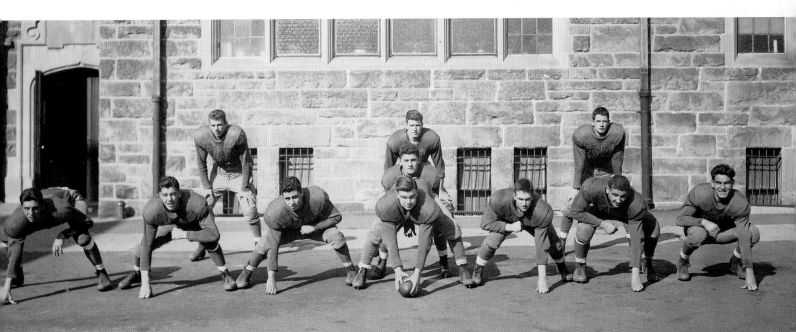

OUR FACULTY

Neal K. Roche

Eugenia Welles

MISS ELIZABETH EMMONS
Religion, Latin, Geometry

MR. NEAL K. ROCHE
English, History, Dramatics

MISS EUGENIA WELLES
Clerk

MR. JOHN P. HEFFERNAN
Instructor of Dancing

MISS ELEANOR CLARKE
Librarian

DR. DAVID GITTERMAN
Athletic Physician

MR. VINCENT O'DONNELL
Instructor of Music

MISS MARY COSGROVE
Librarian

MR. JOHN QUINN
Instructor of First Aid

Andy Palau

Vincent Lombardi

MR. ANDREW PALAU
Mathematics, Physics, Athletic
Coach

MR. VINCENT LOMBARDI
Director of Athletics
Chemistry

Although he knew little about the game, Lombardi's first head coaching job was as basketball coach at St. Cecilia. Taking pointers from colleague and friend Andy Palau, who captained the Fordham basketball team, Lombardi led the Saints to a 10-9 record his first season. *Courtesy of Green Bay Packers Hall of Fame*

lineup at guard and went on to become one of the legendary "Seven Blocks of Granite."

Crowley, a native of Green Bay, Wisconsin, played his high school football under Earl "Curly" Lambeau. It was Lombardi's first encounter with anything connected to Green Bay. After Crowley graduated from East High School he accepted an athletic scholarship to Notre Dame where he became one of the "Four Horsemen"—the Fighting Irish's legendary backfield of Crowley, Harry Stuhldreher, Elmer Layden and Don Miller.

Crowley had a profound impact on Lombardi's playing career, but it's likely he also affected Lombardi's thoughts and opinions on coaching. Lombardi's line coach at Fordham was Frank Leahy, the former Notre Dame star who was on Crowley's staff at Michigan State. Leahy joined Crowley in the move from East Lansing to New York in 1933.

Leahy instilled in Lombardi and his line-mates a methodical, detail-oriented approach that espoused repetition as the path toward perfection. His philosophy emphasized out-executing rather than out-guessing foes.

Lombardi took those lessons to heart, first as a player and then as a coach. His football career at Fordham had to be satisfying on several levels:

• He received top-flight coaching from Crowley and his staff. In fact, the Fordham staff ranked among the finest in the country. Crowley posted a 58-13-7 record during his nine seasons.

• He contributed to a winning team as it was laying the foundation for Fordham's success. Crowley and Lombardi both arrived in 1933, which afforded the incoming freshman a chance to see firsthand how to develop a winning program.

• He developed as a player and realized his full potential

Lombardi served as assistant coach for three years before taking over the head coaching responsibilities at St. Cecilia. The Saints lost their first game under Lombardi, but the team would go undefeated the next 32 games. Lombardi's undefeated 1943 team was the state parochial school champions, giving up only three touchdowns all season. *Courtesy Green Bay Packers Hall of Fame*

because of Crowley's decision to move him from fullback to guard. It may have helped to expand Lombardi's notions about putting players in a position to succeed, rather than giving in to stereotypes and preconceptions.

Although they were not the first to be called the nickname, Lombardi and his fellow offensive linemen became the most famous "Seven Blocks of Granite" when school publicist Tim Cohane dusted off the name used several years before. The group featured Leo Paquin, Ed Franco, Nat Pierce, Alex Wojciechowicz, Lombardi, Al Babartsky and Jon Druze.

Undoubtedly the greatest disappointment of Lombardi's college career came in his final game: The Rams lost to New York University, 7-6, with a Rose Bowl berth at stake.

Lombardi graduated from Fordham in June of 1937 with a Bachelor of Science degree. He narrowed his career choices

to teaching, business or law. While he tried to find his path he worked as a bill collector for a finance company, a job he found distasteful and left after one year.

In 1938, he enrolled in Fordham Law School but withdrew after one semester. The academic standards were too much for Lombardi.

After a brief stint as a chemist at DuPont Chemical Company in Wilmington, Delaware, Lombardi received a call from former Fordham classmate "Handy" Andy Palau, now the head football coach at St. Cecilia High School in Englewood, New Jersey, informing Lombardi of a teaching/coaching vacancy there. Lombardi jumped at the opportunity.

He taught and coached at St. Cecilia's for eight years. From 1939 to 1947, Lombardi developed a solid reputation as a stern but fair educator. He earned an annual salary of $1,700. To cut

Lombardi (fourth from left) was an assistant football coach at the United States Military Academy at West Point starting in 1948 until 1952. He credited Coach Earl "Red" Blaik (center), considered the best college coach of the times, for teaching him how to organize, discipline and inspire a football team.

Photo by U.S. Military Academy/Getty Images

expenses he and Palau shared a room at the boarding house across the street from the school at $1.50 each per week.

In addition to developing into a fine teacher, Lombardi was gaining widespread notoriety as an outstanding coach. His days at St. Cecilia's, he would later say, were among the happiest of his life.

When he began at St. Cecilia's he was a bachelor who liked to play cards, laugh heartily and occasionally have a drink or two. Lombardi was a man's man whose larger-than-life persona took root at St. Cecilia's. Lombardi worked hard and he played hard, sometimes at the same time.

Merv Hyman, a sportswriter for the *Englewood Press*, developed a friendship with Lombardi.

"We used to sit around and drink beer," Hyman said, "and when we got to 22 cans, we'd set up an offense and a defense and run through football plays. All Lombardi talked about, all he

Lombardi was paid $7,000 a year at West Point, with free housing included. *Courtesy Green Bay Packers Hall of Fame*

thought about was football."

Obviously Palau never regretted his decision to recommend Lombardi to St. Cecilia's, where they joined forces to build a high school powerhouse.

Once, Palau asked Lombardi to give the team's customary pregame pep talk. Lombardi's words incited the players and put them in the proper mindset. "He was absolutely fantastic," Palau said in Vince, adding, "At that first pep talk of Lombardi the gymnasium shook."

One player was quoted as saying, "He'd get you so roused up (that) you'd run through a wall for the man."

When Palau left St. Cecilia to coach at Fordham in 1942, Lombardi became the head coach after serving three years as an assistant. After his first season at the helm, Lombardi's team was recognized among the best in the country.

After five highly successful seasons as St. Cecilia's football coach, and one agonizingly painful decision, he chose to leave for Fordham in 1947 to coach the Rams' freshman football and basketball teams. The following year he served as an assistant coach for Fordham's varsity team coached by Ed Danowski. Numerous accounts suggest Danowski and Lombardi clashed in part because of their contrasting coaching styles. While Lombardi hoped he might one day succeed Danowski he didn't stay long enough to find out.

After the 1948 football season, Lombardi agreed to an assistant coaching job at the U.S. Military Academy at West Point. Lombardi was determined to grow as a coach and he felt confident that West Point's legendary head coach, Col. Red Blaik, would be able to provide an education.

Blaik placed an emphasis on execution through repetition, and it became one of the staples of Lombardi's coaching philosophy. He spent five seasons at West Point, with the first three being extremely successful.

In the spring of 1951, however, a cadet cribbing scandal (a violation of the Cadet Honor Code) resulted in 43 of 45 varsity football players being discharged by administrative order. Blaik might have resigned, but instead he opted to stay the course, a difficult decision that left an impression on Lombardi, who regarded it as a pivotal moment because it taught him perseverance. Furthermore, by observing Blaik's methods he claimed to learn how to organize, discipline and inspire a football team.

Blaik modestly downplayed the compliment, saying, "He may have learned a few things during our years together, but he didn't learn that magnetism at West Point. It was always in him. You don't put magnetism into people."

After five seasons at West Point, Lombardi chose to pursue a career in professional football when he accepted an assistant coaching position with the New York Giants in 1953.

Lombardi's attention to detail was so intense that he once got into a heated debate with Coach Blaik over the proper way to deliver the center's snap to the quarterback. Blaik, whose idea of fun was watching game film, proved to be a perfect mentor for Lombardi during his tenure at West Point. *AP Photo/John Rooney*

3

A GIANT LEAP

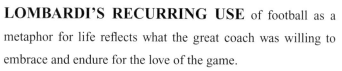

LOMBARDI'S RECURRING USE of football as a metaphor for life reflects what the great coach was willing to embrace and endure for the love of the game.

Those same attributes—perseverance, self-denial, hard work, sacrifice—also reflect what his wife, Marie, was willing to endure not for love of football, but for love of Vince.

Lombardi met Marie Planitz, a tall, attractive blonde from Red Bank, New Jersey, when he was a sophomore at Fordham. It was the fall of 1934, and Lombardi's roommate, Jim Lawlor, introduced him to his cousin, Arthur Planitz, a freshman at Fordham. Planitz invited them to his apartment to meet his family, and Lombardi and Lawlor were glad to tag along. It was there that Lombardi met Marie and their lives changed forever.

She was the only woman Lombardi ever loved; his "first and only girlfriend" according to Lawlor in *When Pride Still Mattered*.

"FOOTBALL IS LIKE LIFE—IT REQUIRES PERSEVERANCE, SELF-DENIAL, HARD WORK, SACRIFICE, DEDICATION AND RESPECT FOR AUTHORITY."

-Vince Lombardi

"Suddenly he plopped into my life and nothing was ever the same," Marie was quoted in *Vince*.

Marie was the daughter of a Wall Street broker, and she fell hard for Lombardi. Despite her father's prejudice-driven disapproval—he didn't want her to marry an Italian—they married August 31, 1940, while Lombardi was teaching and coaching at St. Cecilia's.

During the next 36 years, Vince and Marie had a strong, loving marriage, but it didn't always resemble Hollywood's "and they lived happily ever after" version.

Marie had to deal with the loss of her first child not long after she and Vince were married. That tragedy led her to "drink heavily," according to the Lombardi biography *When Pride Still Mattered*.

In addition, Marie had to deal with an often absent husband. While Lombardi focused on being a terrific coach and top-notch teacher at St. Cecilia's, Marie was left to quietly cope with the loss of a child. The life of a coach's wife had its drawbacks, as Marie knew quite well, saying, "I wasn't married to him more than one week when I said to myself, 'Marie Planitz, you've made the greatest mistake of your life.'"

Marie's drinking may have been exacerbated by Vince's emotional detachment when he was immersed in football, compounded by his own incredible mood swings when he was at home. Still, their marriage seemed to be filled with tremendous passion, emotion and devotion to each other.

There were good times and bad in the Lombardi household, to be

ABOVE: While their life together was at times rocky due in part to Lombardi's mercurial disposition, Vince and Marie's love endured. A photo he gave to Marie reads, "To Rie, The Best Always from Vincent."
Courtesy Green Bay Packers Hall of Fame

LEFT: Vince and Marie were married Saturday, August 31, 1940, at the Church of Our Lady of Refuge in the Bronx. The couple's honeymoon to Maine was cut short when Vince decided to return early so as not to miss the first day of football practice for the St. Cecilia Saints.
Courtesy Green Bay Packers Hall of Fame

sure, but the reasons to celebrate and be grateful far outweighed the rest. Two of the biggest reasons to celebrate were the births of their children. Their son, Vincent Harold Lombardi, was born April 27, 1942. Their daughter, Susan, was born February 13, 1947.

Things changed dramatically, however, when Lombardi accepted a job with the National Football League's New York Giants on December 30, 1953. Lombardi was an assistant under head coach Jim Lee Howell and his responsibilities were similar to today's offensive coordinator. Fellow future Pro Football Hall of Fame coach Tom Landry was Howell's defensive coordinator. Together, Lombardi and Landry were such strong, charismatic, forceful leaders that Howell once joked that his job was to keep order and make sure the footballs were pumped up.

The arrangement seemed to suit Howell's top lieutenants, and the Giants were shaped by and began to thrive under Howell's staff.

Vince and Marie moved from West Point to a brick home in Oradell, New Jersey, in the winter of 1954. Lombardi familiarized himself with the NFL game, which he had never played or coached, by studying game film of the Giants' offense. Vince set up a projector in the den and charted every play, back and forth, until it began driving Marie and the children crazy, so he moved his makeshift office into the basement.

Lombardi quickly identified the Giants' offensive talent: Frank Gifford's smooth-striding gait; Kyle Rote's soft, sure hands; Charlie Conerly's accuracy and quick release.

The Giants had offensive weapons, and Lombardi proceeded

Spurned by West Point, Lombardi's career changed dramatically when he was named an assistant coach of the New York Giants, leaving behind the collegiate world forever. *AP Photo*

to mold them into a formidable attack. While Lombardi retooled the offense, Landry reshaped the defense.

In their third season together, Lombardi and Landry helped lead the Giants to the 1956 World Championship. The Giants defeated the Bears 47-7 on December 30, 1956, at Yankee Stadium.

The success afforded Lombardi the financial security to move his family to Fair Haven, New Jersey, located near Red Bank, where Marie had grown up and some of her relatives still resided. The move pleased Marie and the children, who enjoyed their time and home in Fair Haven.

The Giants finished 8-3-1 in 1956, and a soon-to-be 43-year-old Lombardi felt like it was time to make a move. He had been bypassed several times for college head coaching positions and wondered if he'd ever get a chance.

Lombardi believed his Italian heritage and dark complexion led to prejudice college officials against him. For instance, he sent a letter to Notre Dame after head coach Terry Brennan was fired in December of 1958. Lombardi claimed the letter went unanswered.

He applied for head coaching positions at Southern Cal, Washington, Stanford and the Air Force Academy but "nothing ever happened," a depressed Lombardi told friends.

OPPOSITE: Although he had hoped for the head coaching position with the Giants, Lombardi joined Tom Landry (left) as perhaps the greatest duo of assistant coaches in pro football history. With Lombardi running the offense and Landry controlling the defense, Coach Jim Lee Howell (center) joked that his main job was to make sure there was enough air in the footballs. *Fred Morgan/NY Daily News Archive via Getty Images*

Under Lombardi's guidance, the Giants offense in 1958 averaged more than 20 points a game while finishing 9-3 and earning the right to play the Baltimore Colts for the league title. Lombardi is shown here with fullback Mel Triplett, quarterback Charley Conerly, left halfback Phil King and right halfback Alex Webster. *AP Photo*

That finally changed after the 1957 season. By then, Lombardi's talent and ability were held in high esteem among the NFL's inner circle, and he became a serious head coaching candidate.

The Philadelphia Eagles fired Hugh Devore after a disastrous 1957 season and sought to hire Lombardi away from the Giants. It appeared Lombardi would indeed become the Eagles' head coach until Giants owner Wellington Mara changed Lombardi's mind at the 11th hour. Mara explained that the Eagles' guarantee of a one- or two-year contract wouldn't give him enough time to build a winner. Further, he wasn't afforded the title general manager so he didn't have final say on all personnel decisions. This, Mara believed, would effectively tie Lombardi's hands and make it that much more difficult to succeed there.

Also, Marie was dead-set against moving to Philadelphia and she let Vince know how she felt. Ultimately, Lombardi was forced to agree with Marie and Mara, and he stayed with the Giants for the 1958 season.

It has been hailed as "The Greatest Game Ever Played." Unfortunately for the Giants and Lombardi, New York lost the 1958 NFL Championship game to the Baltimore Colts 23-17 when Alan Ameche (35) scored the winning touchdown in overtime at Yankee Stadium. The game featured 17 future members of the Pro Football Hall of Fame. *Hy Peskin/Sports Illustrated/Getty Images*

After an inauspicious start it proved to be among the most famous seasons in team history. The Giants started 2-2 before finding their stride. They won eight of nine games and found themselves playing the Baltimore Colts for the 1958 NFL Championship at Yankee Stadium, in what many consider the greatest NFL game ever played.

Trailing 17-14 with two minutes to play, Johnny Unitas drove the Colts for the game-tying field goal. The Colts won 23-17 when Alan Ameche scored on a 1-yard run in overtime, which led one sportswriter to coin the phrase, "Sudden Death!"

The game proved transformative for the NFL. It attracted a national television audience and captured the collective attention of the nation. As a result, pro football exploded across the country in the following years. By the mid-1960s, professional football surpassed baseball to become the nation's favorite sport to watch and has remained on top ever since.

History would show that Lombardi's role in the emergence of football as America's game of choice was huge. But the young coach could not see that after the crushing loss coupled with being discounted as a head coaching candidate. It was starting to take its toll on Lombardi until two prominent positions suddenly became a possibility.

West Point's Blaik had stepped down, and it was widely assumed Lombardi would receive his support. However, the athletic board followed tradition and hired a West Point graduate, Dale Hall, for the job.

Lombardi was disappointed, but he shifted his focus to the Green Bay Packers, who were searching for a head coach and a general manager and had shown interest in him.

The once formidable Packers were reeling from 13 straight losing seasons, and the 1958 campaign was a 1-10-1 disaster. New York sportswriter Red Smith, who had grown up in Green Bay, famously quipped: "The Packers underwhelmed 10 opponents, overwhelmed one, and whelmed one."

The height of embarrassment occurred November 2 when the Packers lost to the Colts, 56-0, in Baltimore. Coach Raymond "Scooter" McLean resigned December 17, 1958, under pressure after leading the Packers to the worst record in team history. Team president Domenic Olejniczak sought a "dominant personality" in the general manager's role, and asked seven board members to act as a screening committee for the hiring search.

Iowa's Forrest Evashevski appeared to be a leading candidate, but after visiting Green Bay he elected to stay in Iowa City. Blanton Collier, Kentucky's head coach, and Otto Graham, the former Cleveland Browns quarterback, were also strongly considered.

Ultimately, the search committee centered on Lombardi, who had glowing references from many in the NFL's inner circle, including Paul Brown and George Halas.

The Packers interviewed Lombardi on January 26, 1959, and offered him a dual position as coach and general manager that paid $36,000 annually for five seasons. It included other bonuses and incentives, and Lombardi agreed to the deal.

On January 28, 1959, the Packers announced Vincent Thomas Lombardi as the franchise's head coach and general manager. Lombardi was thrilled. It wasn't long before Green Bay and its fans were ecstatic, too.

Lombardi packs in his hotel in New York, January 28, 1959, after being named head coach and general manager of the Green Bay Packers. His wizardry as offensive coach for the Giants won him his first head coaching assignment above the high school level. AP Photo/Matty Zimmerman

After being named head coach and general manager of the Packers, Lombardi is shown with his family leaving Fair Haven, New Jersey, January 31, 1959. With him is his wife, Marie; daughter, Susan, 12, and son, Vincent, Jr., 17. Even though they arrived in the dead of winter, Green Bay warmly welcomed the Lombardis, and the winning that followed their arrival. *AP Photo/Martin Cohn*

4 BUILDING A DYNASTY

THE GREEN BAY PACKERS' executive committee sought a strong, forceful football man to be the team's new head coach and general manager. Lombardi did not disappoint.

A proud Packers president Domenic Olejniczak announced the selection of Vincent Thomas Lombardi on January 28, 1959. The news immediately drew praise from NFL insiders such as league commissioner Bert Bell, and legendary coaches George Halas of the Chicago Bears and Paul Brown of the Cleveland Browns.

In Wisconsin, the media heartily approved of the hiring and two members of the Packers' executive committee—Green Bay realtor Richard Bourguignon and former Packers star Tony Canadeo—struck up quick and long-lasting friendships with Lombardi.

Any doubts or concerns about Lombardi's motives, goals and commitment to winning were addressed immediately. Following the new coach's first day on the job, a headline in the *Milwaukee Journal* pronounced "Coach Lombardi Takes Full Command of Packers." Lombardi set the tone for his career in Green

"I'VE NEVER BEEN ASSOCIATED WITH A LOSER, AND I DON'T EXPECT TO BE NOW."
-Vince Lombardi

1959 • 1:06 P.M.

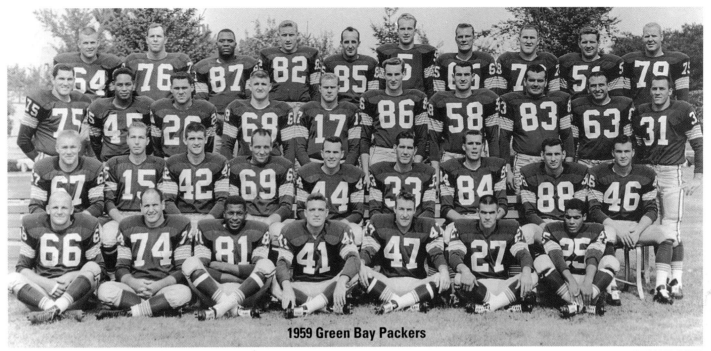

1959 Green Bay Packers

FRONT ROW (from left): Ray Nitschke, Henry Jordan, A.D. Williams, Bob Freeman, Jesse Whittenton, John Symank and Tim Brown. SECOND ROW: Andy Cvercko, Bart Starr, Don McIlhenny, Bill Forester, Bobby Dillon, Lew Carpenter, Gary Knafelc, Ron Kramer and Hank Gremminger. THIRD ROW: Forrest Gregg, Emlen Tunnell, Joe Francis, John Dittrich, Lamar McHan, Boyd Dowler, Dan Currie, Bill Quinlan, Fuzzy Thurston and Jim Taylor. BACK ROW: Jerry Kramer, Bob Skoronski, Nate Borden, Jim Temp, Max McGee, Paul Hornung, Tom Bettis, Norm Masters, Jim Ringo and Dave Hanner.

Bay instantly. He rented a house, hired two assistant coaches, reappointed the front-office personnel, ordered remodeling of the South Washington Street offices, addressed the board of directors, met with the media and attended several other meetings, all in the first 24 hours.

Further, Lombardi spelled out his authority that first day at a noon luncheon with the executive committee members at the Northland Hotel in Green Bay.

"I want it understood that I'm in complete command," he started. "I expect full cooperation from you people, and you will get full cooperation from me in return. You have my confidence, and I want yours."

If anyone on the committee had any lingering doubts, Lombardi boldly set them to rest when he told them, "I've never been associated with a loser, and I don't expect to be now."

Notably impressed, *Milwaukee Journal* sports editor Chuck Johnson wrote "(Lombardi) is calmly confident and efficient. He knows what he wants and he has no doubt that he will get it."

Lombardi began getting what he wanted by assessing the Packers' current roster and deciding who could and could not help the team win. This required a man of vision who knew what his team would look like, and how an individual player's skill would fit into the overall scheme. That Lombardi did so without prejudice set him apart.

He wanted the best football players, not

Lombardi held a quarterbacks camp June 23, 1959, to unveil his offense in Green Bay. From left: Babe Parilli, Bart Starr, Boyd Dowler, Bob Webb, Joe Francis and Lamar McHan. McHan started the season but Starr emerged as the team's leader after seven games. *AP Photo*

the best white football players, or black football players, or blue football players. He didn't care about the color of a player's skin. He cared about a player's character and ability.

"I will absolutely tell you Coach Lombardi had more to do with diversity in the NFL than any coach ever," said Hall of Fame defensive end Willie Davis. "It wasn't just about getting more black players. It was about putting—on the field—the best team that you could with the best players you could get. I would say at Green Bay it was all about the 43 football players the coach could get."

Davis said Lombardi's feeling toward racism of any kind could be summed up in two words: zero tolerance. Whether it was prejudice against any group, Lombardi would have none of it.

"I can tell you truthfully that more than a few players were shown out of Green Bay because they weren't buying in," said Davis, an African-American. "Coach Lombardi approached it with such honesty and openness that I can tell you, right now, and I played for (famed Grambling Coach) Eddie Robinson and

Paul Brown a couple of years, I have never played for a coach with a greater reason of purpose than Coach Lombardi. It really caused me to want to play."

Lombardi's attitude was rare for a NFL head coach at the height of America's Civil Rights movement in the 1960s. The Washington Redskins still had a color barrier in 1960, and other teams also were slow to sign black players, but Lombardi told scouting director Jack Vainisi "to ignore the prejudices then prevalent in most NFL front offices in (Green Bay's) search for the most talented players."

Lombardi's acumen as a talent scout is often underrated. He had the ability to project not only whether a player had the necessary ability, but how that player's skills would fit into the team.

Davis was a perfect example. Selected in the 15th round of the 1956 NFL Player Draft by Cleveland, Davis languished with the Browns as a miscast offensive tackle. Lombardi saw in the cat-quick Davis the ideal defensive end and traded for him.

"I consider speed, agility and size to be the three most important attributes in a successful lineman," Lombardi told Davis in an impassioned telephone conversation. "Give me a man who has any two of those dimensions and he'll do okay. But give him all three and he'll be great. We think you have all three."

"He absolutely would not get off the phone until I promised I would come to Green Bay," Davis said. "Coach Lombardi said, 'Now, Willie, are you going to come to Green Bay?' And I gave him a soft answer. He said, 'No, you're going to come to Green Bay and play left end for us.' Well, I went to Green Bay. I can honestly say when I picked up the phone I had no idea I'd

RIGHT: Willie Davis (87), Jim Taylor (31) and Willie Wood (24) all developed under Lombardi to propel the Packers to football dominance in the 1960s. *AP Photo*

OPPOSITE: With a keen eye for talent and the ability to get the best out of it, Lombardi quickly surrounded himself with great players in Green Bay. An example of that is (from left) Jim Ringo, Boyd Dowler, Ron Kramer, Bart Starr and Jim Taylor. Ringo, Starr and Taylor are now members of the Pro Football Hall of Fame. *Courtesy of Green Bay Packers Hall of Fame*

CHICAGO
BEARS

Official Program

PRICE
25¢

—VS.—

GREEN BAY
CITY STADIUM

GREEN BAY
PACKERS

SEPTEMBER 27th, 1959 • 1:06 P.M.

be going to Green Bay by the time I hung it up."

Davis repaid Lombardi mightily for his belief in him. From 1960 to 1969 Davis anchored the Packers' defensive line while playing in six NFL title games and two Super Bowls. Davis never missed a game in his career, earning Pro Bowl honors five times. He was inducted into the Pro Football Hall of Fame in 1981.

Willie Wood was an undrafted free agent quarterback from Southern California who in 1960 wrote letters to every NFL team requesting a tryout. Lombardi worked out and signed Wood to a contract. Then he moved Wood to defense. As a free safety, Wood was an opposing quarterback's worst nightmare, grabbing 48 interceptions during a Hall of Fame career. Wood, an eight-time Pro Bowl defender, also returned 187 punts for 1,391 yards and two touchdowns during his 12-year career with the Packers.

In 1960, Bob Jeter was drafted in the second round by Lombardi, who liked his athleticism and attitude. Jeter was a halfback at Iowa, where he rushed for a Rose Bowl record 194 yards on nine carries against Cal. Lombardi switched the 6-foot-1, 200-pound halfback to cornerback, where he played 11 seasons. Jeter finished with 26 interceptions for 333 yards and two touchdowns in 11 seasons.

In 1961, Herb Adderley was chosen by Lombardi with the 12th overall pick in the draft. Adderley was an all-America halfback at Michigan State, but he played sparingly behind the Packers' tandem of Paul Hornung and Jim Taylor. But when defensive back Hank Gremminger was injured midway through the season, Lombardi moved Adderley to left cornerback. The decision was pure genius.

Adderley used his exceptional speed, ball skills and size to become one of the NFL's greatest ball-hawking cornerbacks. He finished with 48 career interceptions, including seven for touchdowns.

In 1963, Lombardi used the 14th pick to draft Dave Robinson out of Penn State. Robinson was a tight end/defensive end at Penn State. Lombardi coveted Robinson, but he didn't need a tight end (he had All-Pro Ron Kramer) and he didn't need a defensive end (he had Willie Davis and Lionel Aldridge). He moved Robinson

Fans mob Lombardi after the Packers upset the Chicago Bears 9-6 in Lombardi's first game as Green Bay's coach on September 27, 1959, at City Stadium in Green Bay. *Vernon Biever/Getty Images*

to left outside linebacker where he took over for Dan Currie as the starter in 1964.

Robinson, an effective but seldom used blitzer, had 21 interceptions and joined Ray Nitschke and Lee Roy Caffey to create one of the NFL's greatest linebacker units of all time.

Davis, Adderley and Wood are enshrined in the Pro Football Hall of Fame. Robinson and Jeter are widely regarded as being among the best at their position in that era. All are black players who switched positions and became stars under Lombardi's direction.

Lombardi quickly built a powerful team on both sides of the ball. The Packers' great defenses of the 1960s were menacing. While they never earned a pithy nickname like the Fearsome Foursome of the Los Angeles Rams, or the Dallas Cowboys Doomsday Defense, or even Pittsburgh's Steel Curtain, Green Bay's defensive units were just as formidable.

Henry Jordan, the Pro Football Hall of Fame tackle, teamed with Ron Kostelnik to anchor the line. Davis and Aldridge were

1032 So. Jackson
Green Bay Wis.
Oct. 11, 1960

Dear Mr. Lombardi,

Everybody in our class is happy to know that you go to Mass every day. We are also very happy to know that the Packers won. In our class we have a skrine of all the Packers with you in front of Blessed Mother. I hope you will come and see it some day. It will be a pleasure to have you. Sister will be very happy to see you.

Truly yours,
Anne Gerlach

The Packers, it has been said, are a religion in Green Bay. Lombardi was reminded of that when, as part of a class project, he received a stack of letters from students at St. Willebrord's Catholic School in Green Bay.

Courtesy of Green Bay Packers Hall of Fame

1202 E. Hazel
Green Bay, W
Oct. 10, 1960

Dear Mr. Lombardi

Mr. Lombardi we do like the game you played on Sunday. We think the Packers are wonderful this year. Will you pleace send me and sister your autogafeh and the Packers? We the children of St. Willebrord's 5th and 6th grade invite you and your wife to come to our school and vist us and the other grades too. Hope your Packers win every game and take 1st place in the pro-football league.

Love,
Michael Picard

Handwritten plays by Lombardi while in Green Bay

Lombardi awarded the wives of players after every championship the team won. After the Packers won their first title in 1961 he gave the wives fur stoles. *George Silk//Time Life Pictures/Getty Images*

On offense, Lombardi recognized Starr's limitations as a passer, but realized the studious, serious-minded quarterback possessed incredible leadership skills. Starr's ability to be the coach on the field, and to adroitly execute the game plan, was priceless to Lombardi.

As former *Green Bay Press-Gazette* sportswriter and Packers' public relations man Lee Remmel observed more than once, "Bryan Bartlett Starr would carve up defenses with the precision of a surgeon."

Starr, a 17th-round draft pick in 1956, possessed the football IQ to execute Lombardi's game plans, and the mental toughness to accept the coach's criticism. Starr noted that his father, an Air Force NCO and strong disciplinarian, helped prepare him for his dealings with Lombardi.

Starr was a little-used backup until Lombardi arrived, and even then it took awhile for him to emerge. With five games left in the 1959 season, Starr replaced starter Lamar McHan, leading the Packers to four straight wins to close out the year. Lombardi had found his quarterback. From 1960 through 1967, Starr's won-lost record at quarterback was 62-24-4 and the Packers won six divisional and five NFL titles, as well as the first two Super Bowls. A two-time Super Bowl MVP, Starr was inducted into the Hall of Fame in 1977.

Starr was Lombardi's kind of quarterback because he stayed with the game plan, treated interceptions as anathema and proved to be exceptionally tough and accurate. Starr's career passer rating of 80.5 was second only to Otto Graham (86.6) when he retired after the 1971 season. He remains the only quarterback to win five world championships.

Paul Hornung was treading water when Lombardi arrived. The Notre Dame star and Heisman Trophy winner at quarterback was having trouble finding a position in the pro game. Hornung's reputation as a late-night, carousing bachelor wasn't helping his image. Then Lombardi arrived and saw something special in Hornung. His respect and admiration for "The Golden Boy" was no secret. Neither was the fact that Hornung's talent, versatility and unflinching confidence were keys to the team's success.

the bookends in Green Bay's dominating front four. Nitschke, the Packers' great middle linebacker, was a menacing, larger-than-life figure on the field whose vicious hits set the defensive tone. Lombardi, who admittedly relished football's physical nature, surely appreciated Nitschke's rugged, relentless style.

Nitschke was the first defensive player from the Glory Years to be inducted into the Pro Football Hall of Fame. He finished with 25 career interceptions, a testament to his athleticism.

Quarterback Bart Starr once called Nitschke "a classic example of Dr. Jekyll and Mr. Hyde" because he was so ferocious on the field and so gentle off it. Lombardi could count on Mr. Hyde showing up each Sunday.

RIGHT: Lombardi was the face of professional football, according to Time.

BELOW: The 40th anniversary Time Magazine Dinner in May 1963 brought together three of sports biggest names: Vince, baseball's Casey Stengel and heavyweight champion Joe Louis.

Courtesy of Green Bay Packers Hall of Fame

BOTTOM: Vince and Marie at the Time event in which 284 subjects of the magazine's cover stories were celebrated at the Waldorf-Astoria in New York.

Courtesy of Green Bay Packers Hall of Fame

TWENTY-FIVE CENTS

DECEMBER 21, 1962

THE SPORT OF THE '60s

TIME
THE WEEKLY NEWSMAGAZINE

GREEN BAY COACH
VINCE LOMBARDI

Boris Chaliapin

VOL. LXXX NO. 25
(REG. U.S. PAT. OFF.)

Hornung was renowned for his outrageous lifestyle, but it was his willingness to work and to lead that made Lombardi proud.

Hornung had a nose for the end zone, and Lombardi deployed him accordingly. Hornung scored 72 touchdowns during his Hall of Fame career,. The halfback-kicker totaled a league-record 176 points in the 12-game 1960 season. Lombardi called Hornung "the greatest clutch player" he ever coached.

At fullback, Lombardi deployed the physical and punishing Jim Taylor, whose style was exactly what Lombardi looked for in his fullback. The future Hall of Fame back was a runaway locomotive that produced five straight 1,000-yard rushing seasons. Lombardi said, "Jim Brown will give you that leg and then take it away from you. Jim Taylor will give it to you and then ram it through your chest."

Taylor's fierce style provided an element of toughness on offense that was similar to what Nitschke's rugged brand brought to the defense. The offensive line remained largely the same under Lombardi. It featured: Bob Skoronski, left tackle; Fuzzy Thurston, left guard; Ken Bowman, center; Jerry Kramer, right guard; and Forrest Gregg, right tackle. "Forrest Gregg is the finest player I ever coached," Lombardi said. Gregg, a nine-time Pro Bowl selection and Pro Football Hall of Famer, starred for 15 seasons as a tough, tenacious and undersized (6-4, 249) technician. He is regarded as one of the NFL's greatest at his position.

Lombardi, the old lineman, valued his offensive line and strived for flawless execution from it. Gregg, the very best of a dominant unit, almost always delivered without fail. When injuries along

Lombardi's message to his players. *Photo by Vernon Biever/Getty Images*

the line forced Gregg to play guard for a stretch in 1965, he was selected "all-league" at guard by one major wire service, and "all-league" at tackle by another. He also appeared in a then-record 158 straight games from 1961-67.

Kramer and Thurston powered the Packers' feared power sweep. While Kramer was one of the Packers' most talented players, Thurston was one of the most resilient. Each served Lombardi's greater purpose.

Kramer's strength and athleticism—coupled with Thurston's grit and reliability—created one of the NFL's greatest guard tandems. They also were a great example of Lombardi's insight into players' psyche.

Whereas Lombardi frequently encouraged Kramer, he routinely chastised Thurston. The story goes that Lombardi did so because he realized it was what each needed to succeed. Kramer, a bit of a self-promoter, sought his coach's approval and tended to sulk if he didn't get it. Thurston, the self-deprecating one, rationalized that Lombardi berated him in front of teammates because the coach knew he could take it.

Together, Kramer and Thurston enabled Starr, Hornung and Taylor to become the only Hall of Fame offensive backfield in NFL history.

Tight end Ron Kramer, a multi-sport star at Michigan and a member of the College Football Hall of Fame, also played a key role in the offense. Kramer, as the tight end, was responsible for executing the key block in the sweep. Carroll Dale, Boyd Dowler and Max McGee were the main receivers under Lombardi, who preferred receivers with good size, good hands and good route-

Jim Taylor (31) breaks through the arm-tackles of New York Giants linebacker Sam Huff (70) and defensive tackle Rosey Grier (76) during the 1962 NFL Championship Game, which the Packers won 16-7 at Yankee Stadium. The 1962 Packers dominated, leading the league in scoring with 415 points while giving up a league-low 148 points on their way to a 13-1 record and their second consecutive championship. *Photo by Vernon Biever/Getty Images*

running ability. A desire to block wasn't optional.

Lombardi instilled in his players a belief that they would win.

"That's one of the things I'll always remember," Davis said. "He was so confident we would become winners. He told me that in our first conversation and he meant it. He said, 'Willie, let me tell you one thing: We're going to be winners.' He said it with such force and strength and clarity—with such single-mindedness of purpose—that I believed it."

On July 23, 1959, before the start of training camp, Lombardi addressed his players in a deep, gravelly voice that resonated with authority.

"Gentlemen," he began, "we're going to have a football team. We are going to win some games. Do you know why? Because you are going to have confidence in me and my system … By being alert you are going to make fewer mistakes than your opponent … By working harder you are going to out-execute, out-block (and) out-tackle every team that comes your way."

When the meeting was finished, Starr immediately called his wife, Cherry, and said, "Honey, we are going to begin to win."

Lombardi unveiled his 1959 team in a hard-fought 9-6 victory against Halas' Bears in front of 32,150 fans at City Stadium in Green Bay. Lombardi's team followed it up with back-to-back victories to make it a 3-0 start. The Packers lost five straight but, with Starr under center, finished strong at 7-5, which was good for third place in the Western Conference.

Lombardi was voted professional Coach of the Year in a landslide. Meantime, his former boss, New York Giants owner Wellington Mara, was thinking about replacing head coach Jim

Green Bay Packers

349 SOUTH WASHINGTON STREET | GREEN BAY, WISCONSIN | HEmlock 2-4873

January 4, 1963

Mr. & Mrs. Hank Gremminger
9928 Lakemere Drive
Dallas 18, Texas

Dear Hank & Shirley:

Words could never express my gratitude for your accomplishments of the past season. Our victory in the Championship Game was particularly pleasing since it meant so much to me personally.

I believe you realize now that success is much more difficult to live with than failure. I don't believe anyone realizes, except ourselves, the obstacles we had to face week after week. This, of course, made our season more gratifying.

I was extremely proud of our conduct during the Championship Game. We never lost our poise under what were very trying conditions. The Giants tried to intimidate us physically, but in the final analysis we were mentally tougher than they were and that same mental toughness made them crack.

Character is the perfectly educated will and you are men of character. Our greatest glory was not in never falling, but in rising when we fell.

I hope you both enjoy the TV or stereo. Best wishes to you both and a very happy New Year. Remember, "There is no substitute for victory."

Sincerely,

Vince Lombardi
Head Coach & General Manager

VL:lsk

MEMBER CLUB NATIONAL CONFERENCE AND NATIONAL FOOTBALL LEAGUE • SIX TIMES WORLD CHAMPIONS
TWO TIMES WESTERN DIVISION CHAMPIONS • 1938 - 1960

1929
1930
1931
1936
1939
1944

LEFT: Lombardi, whose relationship with his loved ones was often complicated, enjoys the simple pleasure of handing out Christmas presents to his family. From right, Marie, grandsons Vincent II and John, son Vincent and wife Jill, daughter Susan and her boyfriend Paul Bickman.

BELOW LEFT: In the den of their modest brick home at 667 Sunset Circle in Green Bay, the Lombardis – Vince, Marie and daughter Susan – enjoy an evening of watching TV in 1962.

BELOW RIGHT: Lombardi was more comfortable using a charcoal grill than he was helping Marie in the kitchen. But that didn't keep him from giving her advice.

Photos Courtesy of Green Bay Packers Hall of Fame

GETTYSBURG
OCT - 7 '64
PA.

AIR MAIL

Mr. Vince Lombardi
Coach
The Green Bay Packers
Green Bay, Wisconsin
ARAM PUBLIC LIBRARY
404 E. Walworth Ave.
Delavan, WI 53115

Lee Howell. Mara approached the Packers about Lombardi's availability, and Olejniczak even allowed him to talk to the Giants, but nothing came of it. Ultimately, the Packers rewarded Lombardi for a job well done—and his decision to stay—with a $10,000 bonus. He bought Marie a mink coat.

The Packers built on their success and in 1960 surprised the NFL by going 8-4 to capture first place in the Western Conference. Green Bay met the Philadelphia Eagles for the NFL Championship on December 26 at Franklin Field. The Packers out-played the Eagles but lost 17-13 in a game that was close to the final play. In the waning moments, the Packers drove the field but fell short when Taylor was tackled by linebacker Chuck Bednarik at the Eagles' 9-yard line as the game ended.

Afterward, Lombardi addressed his team in an even, matter-of-fact tone.

"Perhaps you didn't realize that you could have won this game," he said. "We are men and we will never let this happen again … Now we can start preparing for next year."

Lombardi's Packers never lost another elimination game.

Green Bay owned the NFL and captivated the country by winning consecutive NFL Championships in 1961 and 1962, and as always Lombardi was the catalyst.

In 1961, the Packers went 11-3 to easily outdistance second-place Detroit (8-5) in the Western Conference. Then they atoned for the Eagles' loss by hammering Lombardi's former team, the Giants, by an unceremonious score of 37-0 in front of 39,029 at City Stadium.

In 1962, the Packers were even better, finishing 13-1 to dominate the Western Conference and set up a rematch with the Giants in the NFL Championship game. The Packers won 16-7 in front of 64,892 fans at Yankee Stadium.

Lombardi's popularity soared. During the 1962 season he co-authored the book, *Run to Daylight!* with Wilfred Charles (W.C.) Heinz, a freelance writer who had been a reporter, war correspondent and sports columnist for the New York Sun.

Lombardi's insight into his players was especially intriguing. Here are a few excerpts from *Run to Daylight!*:

Bart Starr: "Tense by nature, because he's a perfectionist. I've never seen him display emotion outside of nervousness. Modest. Tends to be self-effacing, which is usually a sign of lack of ego. You never hear him in the locker room telling 'I' stories. He calls me 'sir.' Seems shy, but he's not. He's just a gentleman. You don't criticize him in front of others."

Paul Hornung: "Can take criticism in public or anywhere. You have to whip him a little. He had a hell-with-you attitude, a defensive perimeter he built around himself when he didn't start out well here. As soon as he had success, he changed. He's still exuberant, likes to play around, but serious on the field. Always looks you straight in the eye. Great competitor who rises to heights."

Jerry Kramer: "Nothing upsets him, so you can bawl him out anytime. He's been near death, but he's happy-go-lucky, like a big kid. Takes a loss quite badly, though …"

Willie Davis: "A hell of a young man. Very excitable under game conditions. A worrier. Before a game he's got that worried look, so I try to bolster his confidence. He's not worried about the team losing—he's got confidence in the team—but he's worried about how Willie Davis will perform … about not letting the team down. In Willie Davis we got a great one."

The 1963 season was supposed to be the Packers' march for a third straight NFL Championship. Instead, it began with Hornung's one-year suspension for his involvement in a betting scandal, and it ended with the Chicago Bears going 11-1-2 to edge the Packers (11-2-1) for the Western Conference crown.

The 1964 season was going to bring a chance for redemption, but a slew of injuries, mediocre play and two one-point losses wrecked the season. The Packers limped in with an 8-5-1 record, good for a distant second behind the 12-2 Baltimore Colts.

A decade that started with such promise was now going sideways, and Lombardi would have none of it. Losing was not an option.

> "NOTHING UPSETS HIM, SO YOU CAN BAWL HIM OUT ANYTIME."
> -Vince Lombardi on Jerry Kramer

5

THE GREATEST CHALLENGE

VINCE LOMBARDI was a coach on a mission in 1965.

Still stinging from the disappointment and embarrassment of the 1964 season—one that ended with a humiliating if meaningless 24-17 loss to St. Louis in the Runner-up Bowl—Lombardi meant to will the Packers back to NFL prominence.

He dealt for kicker Don Chandler and receiver Carroll Dale during the off-season, and while some sportswriters portrayed the Packers as a down-bound team beset by age and attrition, Lombardi's confidence held firm. During a July news conference at the start of training camp, he predicted the Packers would capture the NFL Championship.

"We'll win it," he told reporters. Lombardi was prophetic, but nothing came easy.

The Packers raced to a 6-0 start, but then lost three of five as the offense sputtered mightily. The Bears defeated the Packers 31-10 on Halloween at Wrigley Field, and a week later the

---

"WINNING IS NOT A SOMETIME THING; IT'S AN ALL-TIME THING. YOU DON'T WIN ONCE IN A WHILE, YOU DON'T DO THINGS RIGHT ONCE IN A WHILE, YOU DO THEM RIGHT ALL THE TIME."

-Vince Lombardi

"Character cannot be counterfeited, nor can it be put on or cast off like a garment. Like the markings on wood which are ingrained in the very heart of the tree, character requires time and persistence for growth and development."

MR. LOMBARDI

Lions followed with a 12-7 upset of the Packers at Lambeau Field. Suddenly, the '65 season was at a crossroads.

While the Packers' defense dominated opponents, the offense struggled to find its way. Lombardi wouldn't be deterred. The star backfield of Jim Taylor and Paul Hornung was in decline, so Lombardi cut their workload by a third. He mixed in halfbacks Elijah Pitts and Tom Moore.

Lombardi also relied on Bart Starr's keen mind and accurate right arm to lift the offense out of its slump. Starr responded with an MVP-like season, especially in late-season victories over Minnesota, 24-19, and Baltimore, 42-27, to put Green Bay in the driver's seat. A victory at San Francisco in the regular-season finale would have clinched the Western Conference title.

But again, nothing came easy. The Packers and the 49ers played to a 24-24 tie, setting up a Packers-Colts playoff game for the Western Conference Championship. Green Bay knocked off Baltimore, 13-10, in a classic overtime thriller, on

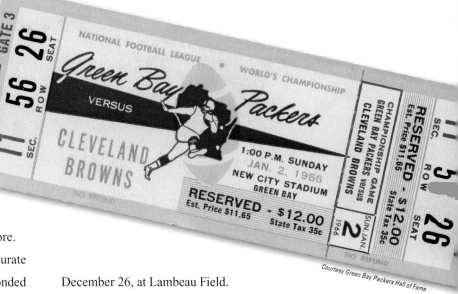

December 26, at Lambeau Field.

On January 2, 1966, the Packers hosted the Cleveland Browns and star running back Jim Brown for the 1966 NFL Championship. The Packers won, 23-12, as 50,777 fans at Lambeau Field saw Don Chandler kick three field goals and Hornung and Taylor combine for 201 yards rushing. Ray Nitschke, the Packers' fierce middle linebacker, harassed and hammered Brown in what proved to be the great back's final game. Brown rushed 12 times for 50 yards. He retired that off-season.

"When I look at the highlight reel of that game, and I see me making tackles one-on-one against (Jim) Brown, I even amaze myself," said defensive end Willie Davis.

After scoring a late touchdown, Hornung hollered, "It's just like the good old days!" on his way to the bench. "Did you hear that?" Lombardi repeated gleefully. "It's just like the good old days!"

The victory did much to erase the pain and disappointment of the previous two seasons. It also set the stage for an incredible and improbable run, with Lombardi in full control. Green Bay went 38-9-2 in Lombardi's final three seasons.

"It all begins with (Lombardi)," Jerry Kramer said. "He was the driving force behind those three straight championships. He

Snow and rain turned the field to mud, but the conditions wouldn't slow fullback Jim Taylor (No. 31 and opposite page) or the Packers, who beat the Cleveland Browns 23-12 in the 1965 NFL Championship Game at Lambeau Field. *Vernon Biever/Getty Images; Color photo: Tony Tomsic/Getty Images*

wouldn't allow us to give anything less than our best. And we didn't want to disappoint."

Lombardi knew what his players, and especially his veterans, were capable of. He knew their strengths and weaknesses. He knew and pushed their limits. That shared intimate knowledge between player and coach, and of Lombardi's offensive scheme, created a dynamic that was much more complex than it appeared. The cohesion, precision and execution were no simple thing to attain.

Lombardi's Packers just made it look simple.

"George Halas had the great saying, 'We knew what, where and when they were going to do it. We just couldn't do anything about it,' " Kramer said.

Lombardi's success was rooted in execution, but he also was a terrific strategist.

"He was an offensive genius," linebacker Dave Robinson said. "He could be standing off to the side watching practice with (defensive coach) Phil (Bengston), and after a play he could immediately tell you why a play worked, which blocks were missed and who blew their assignments. Now, he didn't know the intricacies of defense like Phil did, but he didn't miss much."

Robinson said the defense rarely met with Lombardi, who allowed Bengston great freedom to coach the unit. But when Lombardi did address the defense, it usually wasn't good.

Davis said defensive players would motivate each other with reminders that a subpar effort could earn them a meeting with the coach. The truth, Davis said, was that the players already felt bad.

"When we lost, it was painful, and when we lost, I thought of him first before my own problems with it," he said. "And that's why in my opinion we became winners. We were a team. There was nothing attractive to us about losing, and if there was he made it quickly dissipate."

The challenges during the 1965 season, Davis said, made winning the championship even sweeter. "Coach (Lombardi) really pushed us that season," Davis said. "He poured everything he had into it, and we knew it meant a lot to him (to reclaim the

Even when George Halas' Bears knew what the Packers were doing they often couldn't stop them. Lombardi and Halas last faced each other November 27, 1967. The Packers won 23-17. *Vernon Biever/Getty Images*

OPPOSITE: Wide receiver Boyd Dowler is upended as he scores on a 16-yard pass from Bart Starr in the Packers 34-27 win over the Dallas Cowboys in the 1966 NFL Championship Game on January 1, 1967, at the Cotton Bowl. Lombardi was carried away by the results. *Inset: Russ Russell/Getty Images; Vernon Biever/Getty Images*

championship)."

Lombardi greeted the 1966 season with optimism and an oath.

"I say emphatically—we are not an old football team," he told reporters. "We have experience—and that's what you need to win in this league. Youth is important, certainly, but what you must have is a blend of youth and experience."

The Packers rode that combination of youth and experience to a 12-2 record and the 1966 Western Conference crown. The offense played mostly error-free football with Starr throwing 14 touchdowns to just three interceptions. The defense notched 28 interceptions and 47 sacks while yielding a league-low 163 points.

The Packers' 27-23 victory over the Rams in the regular-season finale summed up this team. Green Bay, at 11-2, had already clinched a berth in the NFL Championship Game. No matter. It still went out and won.

"Sometimes I think no game we ever played for Coach Lombardi gave him as much satisfaction as the one we didn't have to win but did," Starr said in *Vince*.

The victory set up a New Year's Day showdown with Dallas in the Cotton Bowl for the NFL Championship. The Packers defeated the Cowboys, 34-27, as defensive back Tom Brown intercepted a fourth-down pass by Dallas quarterback Don Meredith in the end zone to seal the game. In winning, the Packers earned a berth in the first AFL-NFL World Championship, which later became known as Super Bowl I.

The Kansas City Chiefs represented the upstart American Football League, and Lombardi wasn't taking anything for granted. The pressure of carrying the torch for the entire NFL weighed heavily on Lombardi.

"It wasn't only Packer prestige, but the whole NFL (that) was on the line," Lombardi said. "We had everything to lose and nothing to gain."

After a tense first half, Lombardi's Packers responded in a

Kansas City Chiefs cornerback Fred Williamson (24) chases Green Bay receiver Max McGee in what would be known as Super Bowl I, a 35-10 Packers victory on January 15, 1967, at the Los Angeles Memorial Coliseum. *James Flores/Getty Images*

World
Championship
Game
AFL vs. NFL

3 1   10   9
TUNNEL   ROW   SEAT

World Championship Game

Super Bowl I
Ticket

ARAM PUBLIC LIBRARY
404 E. Walworth Ave.
Delavan, WI 53115

After enduring hours of sub-zero temperatures, Packers fans let off steam by tearing down the goal posts following their team's victory.

Vernon Biever/Getty Images

Frank Gifford, who was working as a color analyst on the TV broadcast, famously quipped, "I'm going to take a bite of my coffee."

Ever the disciplinarian, Lombardi banned anyone but offensive linemen from wearing gloves. Lombardi did have his limits: he allowed equipment manager Dad Braisher to hand out long underwear, making sure he took a pair for himself.

The game was a rematch of the 1966 NFL Championship, which the Packers won 34-27 in dramatic fashion. The Cowboys were talented, well coached, and even touted as the team of the future. The cold was just one of Lombardi's concerns.

The greatest obstacle was the Cowboys and their coach, Tom Landry.

Old coaching mates with the Giants in New York, Lombardi and Landry were both extremely competitive. Lombardi took over the Packers in 1959, while Landry joined the expansion Cowboys in 1960. It took Lombardi one year to turn a losing team into a winning team. It took Landry six years before he could say the same.

The outlook was grim for Lombardi and Starr until the final minutes when determination and execution would define the outcome, not the weather. *Vernon Biever/Getty Images*

Such things mattered to Lombardi.

"There's no question it meant a lot (to Lombardi) given their past history with the Giants," Davis said. "Coach always had us well-prepared, but when it came to Tom Landry and the Cowboys it seemed like we were maybe a little bit more prepared than for most teams."

The Packers' preparation helped them do more than cope with the cold.

"He made (the cold) seem like it may be a little inconvenient," Davis said. "But at the end of the day, the Packers would prevail."

That looked to be the case early on. The Packers built a 14-0 lead midway through the second quarter, and it appeared Dallas was no match for the Packers or the cold.

The Packers' first score came on an 8-yard touchdown pass from Bart Starr to Boyd Dowler. It came on Green Bay's opening possession and capped an impressive 82-yard scoring drive. The Packers went up 14-0 when Starr connected with Dowler on a 43-yard touchdown pass early in the second quarter.

Just when it appeared the Packers were going to win in a rout, Dallas' defense rose up with four minutes to play in the half. Starr fumbled when he was hit dropping back to pass, and the Cowboys' George Andrie recovered it and ran 14 yards for Dallas' first score to slice Green Bay's lead to 14-7.

Two minutes later, the Packers' Willie Wood dropped back to field a punt, but one of the NFL's top return specialists fumbled

the ball. The Cowboys recovered and four players later they kicked a field goal to make it 14-10 at halftime. Just like that a potential rout was now anyone's game.

A scoreless third quarter heightened the tension.

Dallas dominated the action, taking its first lead on the first play of the fourth quarter. Meredith handed off to halfback Dan Reeves, who rolled left, stopped and threw an option pass to receiver Lance Rentzel, who got behind the Packers' defense for a 50-yard touchdown.

The Cowboys led 17-14 and it was getting late. The Packers' offense, as right guard Jerry Kramer pointed out, had done little to that point. "As much coverage as there has been on the Ice Bowl not much has been said about our performance before the final drive," Kramer said. "We had something like 10 possessions, 31 plays and a minus 9 yards."

Now, the Packers were down to their final drive.

Green Bay took over at its own 32-yard line with 4:50 to play. On the sideline, Lombardi and Starr discussed strategy and decided to work the football down the field, rather than going for the riskier big play.

Starr began with a 6-yard completion to running back Donny Anderson out of the backfield. Chuck Mercein, playing in only his sixth game with the Packers, rushed for 7 yards to move the chains. Starr hit Dowler for a 13-yard completion to give Green Bay a first down at the Dallas 42.

GREEN BAY'S OVERNIGHT FORECAST called for clear skies and temperatures in the mid-twenties for Sunday's 1 p.m. kickoff at Lambeau Field. ◆ "That'll work," thought the Packers' defensive lineman Willie Davis as he nodded off to sleep.

On the eve of the December 31, 1967, NFL Championship Game between the Dallas Cowboys and the Packers, nobody gave the weather a second thought, unless it was Lombardi.

The Packers' head coach was proud of the electric coils buried six inches beneath the turf at Lambeau Field. The day before the game he acted as tour guide to sportswriters from Dallas and New York in order to show off the $80,000 heating system. Lombardi explained to a riveted audience how the coils heated the turf, making the surface neither too sloppy nor too firm, but just right for optimum safety and footing.

That was when it worked. Not much of anything worked, however, when Arctic cold grabbed hold of Green Bay overnight, forcing temperatures well below zero.

On the morning of the game, Jerry Kramer saw a gas station thermometer that read "minus-6." He simply assumed it was broken. The Packers' All-Pro guard was on his way to the stadium. He knew it was cold, but it couldn't be that cold.

Actually, it was colder by kickoff.

The official game-time temperature was 15 below zero with a wind chill of 36 below. Warmly remembered by NFL historians and fans alike as the "Ice Bowl," the game remains the coldest title game in NFL history.

Played under brutal conditions, the game was not for the timid. When referee Norm Schachter tried blowing his whistle it froze to his lips. The marching band scheduled to play before the game and at halftime cancelled its performance after instruments froze.

BELOW: The Packers jumped to a 14-0 second-quarter lead when Boyd Dowler pulled in a 43-yard touchdown pass from Starr as Mel Renfro stumbled to catch up. Despite the conditions, Dowler caught four passes for 77 yards and two touchdowns. *AP Photo*

THE ICE BOWL

FROZEN IN NFL HISTORY

PLAYED IN MIND-NUMBING COLD, THE 1967 NFL CHAMPIONSHIP GAME DEFINED THE GREATNESS OF BOTH LOMBARDI AND HIS PACKERS.

After Anderson lost 9 yards on a broken running play, he caught passes of 12 and 9 yards to set up the Packers with a first down at the Dallas 30 with two minutes left in the game.

On the next play, Starr lofted a beautiful pass in the icy late afternoon air toward Mercein, who hauled it in for a 19-yard gain. It was a marvelous play under the conditions, setting the Packers up at the Cowboys' 11. Mercein rushed for 9 yards on the next play, and Anderson gained a yard to give Green Bay a first-and-goal at the Dallas 1.

Twice Anderson was given the ball. And twice Dallas stopped him cold. The Packers used their final timeout. Trailing by 3 points, Green Bay faced third-and-goal at the 1 with 16 seconds to play. On the sideline, Lombardi never considered attempting a tying field goal. Starr did all the talking during the timeout. He wanted to run a wedge play, with Mercein running the ball behind center Ken Bowman and Kramer. It made sense. The wedge is the simplest play in football.

"Run it," Lombardi snapped. "And let's get the hell out of here."

The call in the huddle: "31 Wedge." Only after calling it does Starr reconsider. The footing is treacherous. The field is like a skating rink. What if Mercein slips? What if the hole closes before Mercein can reach the end zone?

Starr, Lombardi's trusted field general, considers the risks too great. Without telling anyone, Starr decides to keep the ball himself. A quarterback sneak. A play the Packers don't have in their playbook. A play they never practiced.

On the sidelines, Davis looked away. "I couldn't watch," he said. "It was too nerve-racking."

At the snap, Kramer and Bowman drove Jethro Pugh, the Cowboys' left defensive tackle, off the line. Starr, pushing behind his guard and center, squeezed into the end zone for the winning score. The moment, spontaneous yet decisive, is one of the greatest in NFL history.

When the Lambeau Field crowd of 50,861 rose together to unleash a thunderous roar, Davis knew the Packers were again champions.

Afterward on the drive home, basking in the glow of another championship, Lombardi told his son Vincent that he had just seen his father coach his second-to-last game.

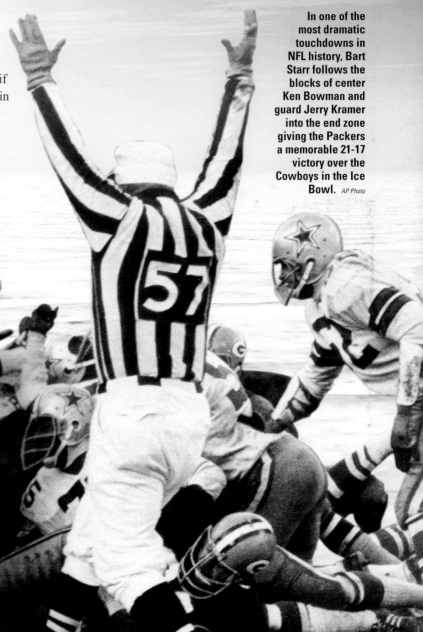

In one of the most dramatic touchdowns in NFL history, Bart Starr follows the blocks of center Ken Bowman and guard Jerry Kramer into the end zone giving the Packers a memorable 21-17 victory over the Cowboys in the Ice Bowl. *AP Photo*

N.F.L. CHAMPIONSHIP GAME
PACKERS vs. COWBOYS
DECEMBER 31, 1967
LAMBEAU FIELD • GREEN BAY, WIS.

PRICE **$1.00**

big way. They rolled to a 35-10 rout of the Chiefs. Afterward, Lombardi was smothered by questions wanting him to compare the NFL and AFL. Finally, he said, "That's a good football team, but it is not as good as the top teams in our league."

In 1967, the goal was apparent, and Lombardi didn't shy away from it.

As the season opened, Lombardi told his players, "Gentlemen, no team in the history of the National Football League has ever won three straight world championships. If you succeed, you will never forget this year for the rest of your lives."

And, he concluded, "Gentlemen, this is the beginning of the big push."

Robinson said every player knew what was at stake entering the 1967 season. "We knew Coach Lombardi wanted that third straight championship," Robinson said. "We wanted it for him. Shoot, we wanted it for ourselves."

The Packers went 9-4-1 to capture first place in the newly formed NFL Central Division, ahead of the Bears (7-6-1), the Lions (5-7-2) and the Vikings (3-8-3).

After the Packers defeated the Bears, 17-13, on November 26 at Wrigley Field, Lombardi and his players didn't feel like

OPPOSITE: Lombardi promised his players they would never forget the 1967 season. Thanks to the team's third straight title, neither did football historians. *Walter Iooss Jr./Sports Illustrated/Getty Images*

BELOW: Lombardi was a perfectionist, a trait that played out during demanding film sessions as the Packers prepared for the Western Conference championship game against the Los Angeles Rams in 1967. *AP Photo/PJS*

celebrating much. According to Davis, they knew there was a tough road ahead, including a date with the Los Angeles Rams in the Western Conference title game.

"Naturally we enjoyed beating the Bears any time, but we knew the season was far from finished," Davis said. "We knew there was a Super Bowl, if we got there, and the NFL Championship Game, of course, but the Rams were also on our minds."

The Packers' wariness served them well in a 28-7 victory

Bart Starr was the hero of the Ice Bowl, to the delight of Packer fans. *Vernon Biever/Getty Images*

over the Rams. Kramer said Lombardi utilized Marv Fleming by lining up the tight end next to right tackle Forrest Gregg. Fleming would block down on the Rams' All-Pro defensive end, Deacon Jones, to neutralize his pass rush. Starr completed 17 of 23 passes and Travis Williams rushed for 88 yards and two touchdowns.

"Magnificent. Just magnificent," Lombardi told his players. "I've been very proud of you guys all year long. You've overcome a great deal of adversity. You've hung in there, and when the big games came around …"

Lombardi couldn't say anything else. He didn't have to.

Eight days later, the Packers played the Dallas Cowboys in the NFL Championship Game in arctic-like conditions at Lambeau Field. In football lore, the game is simply referred to as The Ice Bowl.

Foregoing a tying field goal, the Packers defeated the Cowboys, 21-17, on Starr's 1-yard quarterback sneak with 16 seconds to play and Green Bay trailing 17-14.

"That final drive is still one of the most amazing things in sports," Kramer said. "You look at the offensive statistics from that game. We didn't do anything until that final drive. Why? How could we put it all together at that moment? It's because of (Lombardi). We weren't going to let him down, and we knew it. When Bart came into the huddle, he told us, 'We're going to go down and score the winning touchdown.' Later, I asked Bart how he knew, and he said, 'I knew the instant I looked in your eyes, and (Skoronski's) eyes, and Fuzzy's eyes … I knew we were going to score a touchdown and win.'"

The Ice Bowl victory meant the Packers would represent the NFL in the AFL-NFL World Championship, later known as Super Bowl II.

Lombardi's teams had come far in the past three seasons. The AFL's Oakland Raiders represented all that stood between the Packers and the immortality that comes with winning three straight championships. The pregame speech was vintage Vince. He hit all the right notes the way Sinatra does, and like the great singer, he also did it his way.

"It's very difficult for me to say anything," he told his team before they took the field against the Raiders. "Anything I could say would be repetitious. This is our twenty-third game this year … Boys, I can only say this to you: Boys, you're a good football team. You are a proud football team. You are the world champions. You are the champions of the National Football League for the third time in a row, for the first time in the history of the National Football League. That's a great thing to be proud of.

AFL VS NFL
1968 WORLD CHAMPIONSHIP GAME

Super Bowl II
Ticket

ARAM PUBLIC LIBRARY
404 E. Walworth Ave.
Delavan, WI 53115

**JANUARY 14
ORANGE BOWL
MIAMI, FLORIDA
PRICE $1.00**

"But let me just say this: All the glory, everything that you've had, everything that you've won is going to be small in comparison to winning this one. This is a great thing for you. You're the only team maybe in the history of the National Football League to ever have this opportunity to win the Super Bowl twice. Boys, I tell you I'd be so proud of that I just fill up with myself. I just get bigger and bigger and bigger.

"Head for the dressing room, boys," Lombardi told Forrest Gregg and Jerry Kramer after Green Bay beat Oakland 33-14 in Super Bowl II, Lombardi's last game as Packers' coach. *Vernon Biever/Getty Images*

"It's not going to come easy. This is a club that's gonna hit you. They're gonna try to hit you and you got to take it out of them. You got to be forty tigers out there. That's all. Just hit. Just run. Just block and just tackle. If you do that, there's no question what the answer's going to be in this ball game. Keep your poise. You've faced them all. There's nothing they can show you out there you haven't faced a number of times—Right? Let's go. Let's go get 'em."

The Packers led 16-7 at the half, and future Hall of Fame cornerback Herb Adderley's 67-yard interception return for a touchdown in the fourth quarter preserved the Packers' 33-14 victory over Oakland coach John Madden's Raiders.

Afterward, Lombardi was riding an emotional high. He relished being carried off the field in victory, on the shoulder pads of offensive linemen Forrest Gregg and Jerry Kramer, shouting, "Head for the dressing room, boys."

The scene inside the locker room was one of jubilation and admiration. Lombardi cried, hugged his players and smiled broadly. Life was good.

Oh, there had been hints about retirement, but Lombardi told reporters, "No announcements," when asked about his future. The next day, though, he said, "I really have to sit down for some serious self-conversation and give Vince Lombardi a good, hard look. And I've got to talk to Mrs. Lombardi."

In late January, after Lombardi returned from vacationing in Miami, he informed the Packers' executive committee of his decision to quit coaching. Lombardi planned to stay on as the team's general manager, but his recommendation was for Phil Bengston, his defensive coordinator for nine years, to replace him as head coach.

The official announcement of Lombardi's retirement from coaching came on Thursday, February 1, 1968, during a news conference at the Oneida Golf & Riding Club in Oneida. A dozen TV cameras and more than 100 reporters covered the event, which was broadcast statewide.

Essentially, Lombardi said the dual roles of head coach and general manager were too much for one person. It had become a "seven-days-a-week job the whole year 'round," Lombardi explained. The pressure, the stress and the workload had taken its toll.

Asked if this meant he was committed to not coaching again, Lombardi replied, "Yes, it does."

OPPOSITE: Lombardi's road to glory in Green Bay led to the dedication of Lombardi Avenue on August 7, 1968. Mayor Donald Tillman and Lombardi admire the new road designation during "A Salute to Vince Lombardi Day." *AP Photo*

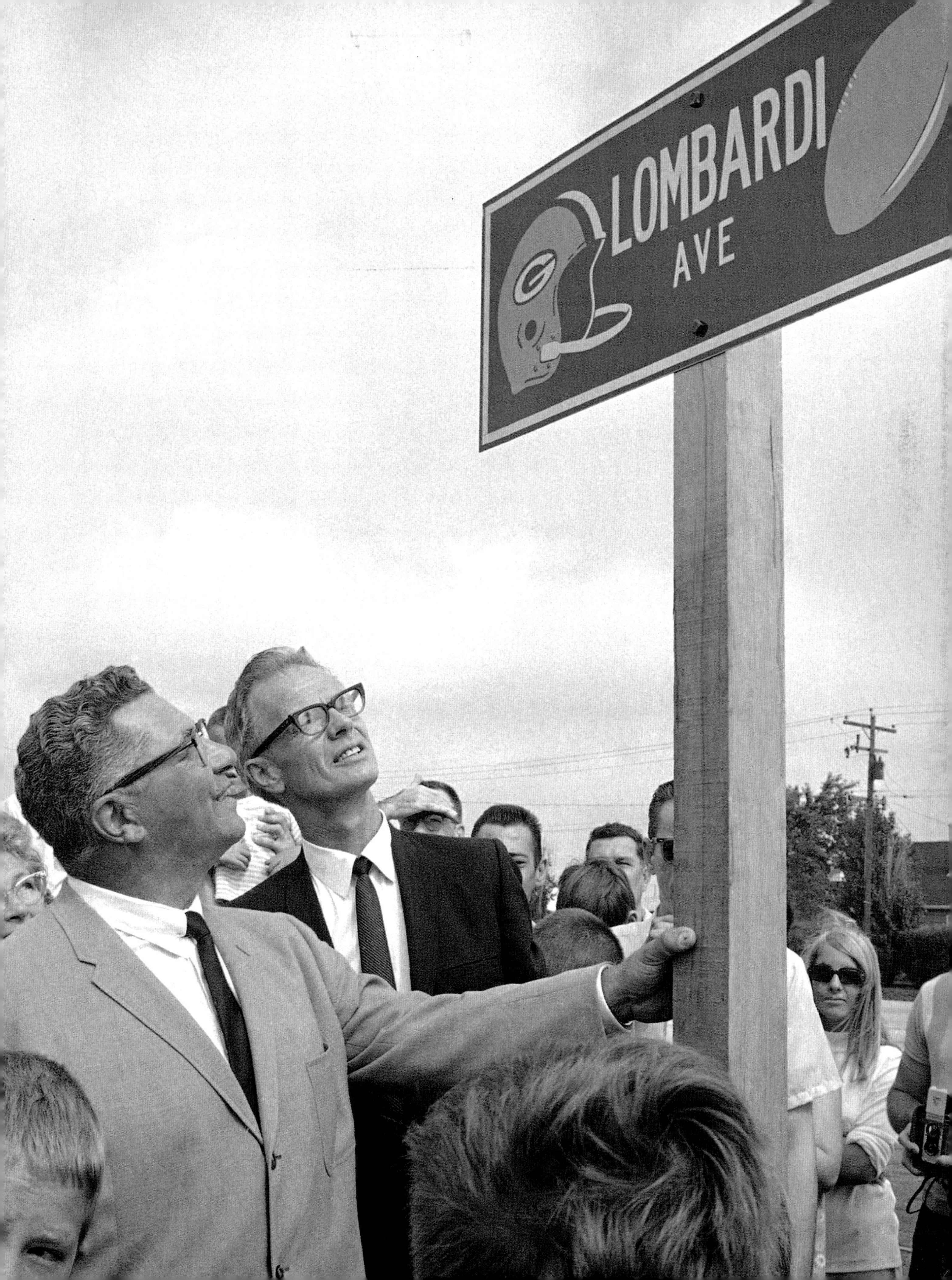
LOMBARDI
AVE

6

A COACH UNTIL THE END

DESPITE HIS BEST INTENTIONS, Lombardi was nothing if not a coach. That became obvious after one thoroughly dissatisfying season as Green Bay's General Manager. After retiring as coach and after watching the Packers falter to 6-7-1 in 1968 under new coach Phil Bengston, Lombardi desperately yearned to return to coaching.

Naturally, he was in great demand, but his relationship with Washington Redskins' owner Edward Bennett Williams and a substantial financial package ended any debate about where he might end up. In February 1969 Lombardi left Green Bay and was hired to lead the Redskins. Lombardi was granted full control of the team with the title of executive vice president and head coach.

Lombardi had an immediate impact on the moribund Redskins. After a modest (by Lombardi's standards) 7-5-2 inaugural

"ANY MAN'S FINEST HOUR—HIS GREATEST FULFILLMENT TO ALL HE HOLDS DEAR—IS THAT MOMENT WHEN HE HAS WORKED HIS HEART OUT IN A GOOD CAUSE AND LIES EXHAUSTED ON THE FIELD OF BATTLE—VICTORIOUS."

-Vince Lombardi

Both Lombardi and the Redskins were rejuvenated by his return to coaching. *Paul Fine/Getty Images*

Watching the Packers play, not from the sidelines but perched in a specially made booth above Lambeau Field, proved unbearable for Lombardi in 1968. *Leonard Mccombe/Time Life Pictures/Getty Images*

OPPOSITE: A humble Lombardi receives the John V. Mara Memorial Sportsman of the year award at the Catholic Youth Organization 33rd Annual Gold Medal Dinner in New York, February 5, 1969. Archbishop Terence J. Cooke of New York presents the award. *AP Photo/John Rooney*

Lombardi rode into Washington with a winner's attitude—something the Redskins dearly needed. *Bob Peterson//Time Life Pictures/Getty Images*

Time mellowed Lombardi, at least when it came to his family. He was much more relaxed with his grandchildren than he had been with his own son. *Nate Fine/Getty Images*

RIGHT: Lombardi was the toast of Washington. Here he is featured in Berry's World, one of America's most widely syndicated editorial cartoons from 1963 to 2003. *Courtesy of Green Bay Packers Hall of Fame*

BELOW: The Redskins rallied around Lombardi, scratching out their first winning season in 14 years. *Nate Fine/Getty Images*

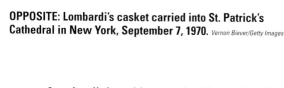
The Vince Lombardi U.S. Stamp was issue June 25, 1977.

OPPOSITE: Lombardi's casket carried into St. Patrick's Cathedral in New York, September 7, 1970. *Vernon Biever/Getty Images*

wove Lombardi into his speech. Nixon described Lombardi as "a man who in a time when so many seem to be turning away from religion was devoutly religious and devoted to his Church; at a time when the moral fabric of the country seems to be coming apart, he was a man who was deeply devoted to his family; at a time when it seems rather square to be patriotic, he was deeply and unashamedly patriotic; at a time when permissiveness is the order of the day in many circles, he was a man who insisted on discipline … discipline and strength."

Shirley Povich, the great *Washington Post* sportswriter, captured the sense of loss in his September 4, 1970, column:

"The Vince Lombardi story has ended too soon, his allotted years too few. A dreaded sickness cut down a man who exceeded his renown as professional football's most distinguished and successful coach. Vince Lombardi transcended the game which made him famous and which he, in turn, honored with the genius he brought to it.

"… In his first and only year as the Redskins' coach, Lombardi walked into a situation that had seethed more than once with sub-surface racial strife. Almost mysteriously, it dissolved in a team brotherhood. Redskin players learned, as the Packers had, that on the practice field Lombardi was a rare mix of harsh and quick disciplinarian and sensitive softie when he learned of a player's limitations. …"

Lombardi's death shook his former players to the core.

Dave Robinson, the Packers' great outside linebacker, compared Lombardi's death to losing his father all over again. Robinson was 15 when his father died of heart disease at 52.

"I refer to Coach and my father in the same breath," Robinson said. "They were both father images to me. When I reached 52, I realized just how young my father was when he died, and it

campaign, fans were energized by the Redskins' first winning season since 1955. They eagerly awaited a second season under Lombardi. As it turned out, it would be a season filled not with victory but of great loss.

On June 15, Lombardi welcomed 62 players to the team's pre-training camp workouts at Georgetown University. A day after camp opened, Lombardi grew so weak during his morning run that he had to stop, which was uncharacteristic. The following evening he almost passed out at a party from extreme exhaustion. Acute constipation and other complications developed in the next several days, forcing Lombardi to see Dr. George Resta, the Redskins' team physician, on June 22. Resta sent Lombardi to Georgetown University Hospital.

A biopsy revealed a fast-growing cancer in Lombardi's colon. On June 27 doctors at Georgetown removed two feet of Lombardi's colon, including a three-centimeter tumor. Lombardi underwent cobalt therapy and chemotherapy, but the cancer was relentless. This was one battle even Lombardi couldn't win.

Vince Lombardi died September 3, 1970. He was 57.

News of Lombardi's death rocked the country. *Time, Newsweek* and other national publications devoted major coverage to the story.

President Richard Nixon, speaking at a White House dinner,

shook me up. Then, when I got to 57, I thought long and hard about how that was only as far as Coach made it. Those feelings of sadness never go away."

As the severity of Lombardi's illness grew more public, many former players traveled to Washington, D.C., to see him for what they feared would be the last time. Willie Davis was among those praying for a miracle.

Giants' owner Wellington Mara informed Davis of the gravity of Lombardi's health at a Giants-Chargers pre-season game in San Diego, which Davis was working as a member of the TV broadcast crew. Davis got on a flight to Washington that night. He was the last of Lombardi's former players to see him alive.

"He was on his deathbed," Davis said. "He was a skeleton."

Bart Starr and Paul Hornung, outside St. Patrick's Cathedral prior to Lombardi's funeral, said they felt as if they had lost a father when their former coach died. *Photo by Vernon Biever/Getty Images*

Davis walked into the hospital room and Lombardi looked at him, grinned broadly, and said, "Willie, you're the best deal I ever made." Then, Lombardi added, "I just want you to know that you were a great player …"

Lombardi broke down before he could finish the sentence, and after a moment to recompose, Davis said he softly asked everyone to leave.

"There's nothing else that has struck me with the impact that the Lombardi situation did," Davis said. "It was very much like how I felt when I lost my mother."

Davis admitted he didn't handle Lombardi's death well.

"It really had me in a low spirit and I was really bothered by it for a long time," he said, pausing to clear the lump in his throat. "To this day, I start talking about it and it draws some emotion."

After Lombardi died, his body lay in a closed casket at Gawler's Funeral Home in Washington for a day, and then it was moved to the Abbey Funeral Home in New York for two days. In Green Bay, more than 2,000 people attended a September 6 service at Veterans' Memorial Arena.

On September 7 more than 3,000 people attended Lombardi's funeral at St. Patrick's Cathedral in New York. At least as many people lined up along Fifth Avenue. Archbishop Terence Cooke, a friend of Lombardi's, delivered the eulogy, quoting St. Paul, "I have fought the good fight to the end. I have run the race to the finish; I have kept the faith."

Davis joined Bart Starr, Paul Hornung, Tony Canadeo, Wellington Mara, Dick Bourguignon, Edward Bennett Williams and Marc Chubb as honorary pallbearers.

After Mass, a 40-limousine procession made the 45-minute drive to Mount Olivet Cemetery in Middletown Township, New Jersey, where Lombardi was buried. He remains there buried next to his wife, Marie, who died of lung cancer in 1982, and his parents, Harry and Matilda.

Truth, honor and hard work breed credibility, and credibility is the currency used by the very best teachers, coaches and managers to motivate their people. Lombardi's sheer force of will and singular purpose created a climate for success. His genius was in devising methods that inexorably linked what was best for the player to what was best for the team.

Together, under Coach Lombardi's direction, his players realized anything was possible, even greatness.

OPPOSITE: Lombardi embraced the words of St. Paul, who in his letter to the Corinthians wrote, "Brethren: Don't you know that while all the runners in the stadium take part in the race, only one wins the prize. Run to Win." *Robert Riger/Getty Images*

ABOUT THE AUTHOR

A writer and sports radio personality, Chris Havel has covered the Green Bay Packers for more than 20 years. He is the author of several Packers-related books, including his work with Brett Favre on the quarterback's autobiography, *Favre: For the Record* (Doubleday, 1997), a *New York Times* best-seller. Havel also collaborated with Bonita Favre, Brett's mother, on the national best-seller, *FAVRE* (Rugged Land, 2004).

On the radio, Havel hosts *Sports Line* on WDUZ 1400-AM and 107.5 FM; the No. 1 rated sports talk show in Northeast Wisconsin. For more than 15 years, Havel covered the Green Bay Packers and was an award-winning columnist for the *Green Bay Press-Gazette*. He was named Wisconsin's Sports Columnist of the Year in 2006 by the Milwaukee Press Club. A Wisconsin native, Havel lives in Green Bay.

ACKNOWLEDGEMENTS

This book would not have been possible without the help and guidance of many wonderful people. A special thanks to the Green Bay Packers Hall of Fame for their unending enthusiasm and assistance on this project, particularly Director/Archivist Tom Murphy, Manager Gwen Borga and Assistant Ashley Nies. Thank you to Packers memorabilia expert Chris Nerat and Packer historian Eric Goska who were always ready to lend a hand at a moment's notice.

BIBLIOGRAPHY

Goska, Eric. *Green Bay Packers: A Measure of Greatness*. Iola, Wis.: Krause Publications, 2004

Hornung, Paul, with Billy Reed. *Lombardi and Me: Players, Coaches, and Colleagues Talk About the Man and the Myth*. Chicago: Triumph Books, 2007

Kramer, Jerry, with Dick Schaap. *Instant Replay*. New York: New American Library, 1968

Kramer, Jerry, with Dick Schaap. *Distant Replay*. New York: Putnam, 1985.

Lombardi, Vince, with W.C. Heinz. *Run to Daylight!* Englewood Cliffs, N.J.: Prentice-Hall, 1963

Maraniss, David. *When Pride Still Mattered: A Life of Vince Lombardi*. New York: Simon & Schuster, 1999

O'Brien, Michael O. *Vince: A Personal Biography of Vince Lombardi*. New York: Morrow, 1987

Robinson, Dave, with Royce Boyles. *The Lombardi Legacy: 30 People Who Were Touched by Greatness*. Goose Creek Publishers, 2009